SOUTHWESTERN DESIGNS

✚

Jeanette Cross

SUNSTONE PRESS

SANTA FE
NEW MEXICO

SOUTHWESTERN DESIGNS ✠ 2

ISBN: 0-86534-047-1

Published by SUNSTONE PRESS
       Post Office Box 2321
       Santa Fe, NM 87504-2321 / USA
       (505) 988-4418 / Orders Only: (800) 243-5644

INTRODUCTION

The southwestern designs in this book are suitable for a variety of craft projects. They can be used for pictures, wall hangings, pillow covers, curtains, bags, rugs and articles of clothing. The designs can be used for all kinds of needlework. They can also be a basis for painting in any media. The repetition of a design or the combination of several will give your project that desired southwestern feeling.

To make your own transfer patterns from this book, use thin tracing paper and a blue transfer pencil. Transfers can be stamped on fabrics.

Basic colors of the Southwest are brown, rust, black, red and yellow. Sometimes these are referred to as "earth" colors. But there are other bright colors associated with this area and one of the most prominent is blue. Blue is the color of turquoise which can range in hue from light blue to a blue-green. It is the stone used most predominantly in Indian jewelry.

When planning your projects remember to use bright colors: red, purple, green, yellow and, of course, turquoise in jewelry and in clothing trim. Southwestern adobe houses made from mud are brown, ranging from light tan to darker shades with blue or green trim on windows and doors.

Traditional Indian pottery designs are tan, black and rust. Modern pottery is very similar but can be various shades of brown with designs in rust, black and white. Some Indian potters add touches of red or blue; others make all black pottery.

Indian dolls, "kachinas," are painted in bright eye-catching colors; red, green and yellow are popular, with accents of black and white.

Whether you are doing applique, embroidery, painting or woodworking, these designs will give you the inspiration and help that results in a happy ending for your hours of work. ✛

Taos Pueblo

Horno / Oven

Ristra / Red Peppers

Navajo Weaver

Navajo Weaving

Buffalo Dancer

Navajo Boy

Navajo Girl

Kachina

Kachina

Rainbow God

Indian Designs

Gambel Quail

Indian Symbols

Hogan

Lightning

Rain

Deer Track

Mountain

Corn

Bird

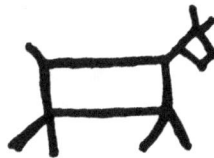
Horse

Sun

Bean Sprout

Butterfly

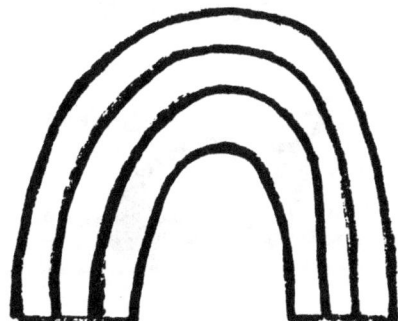
Rainbow

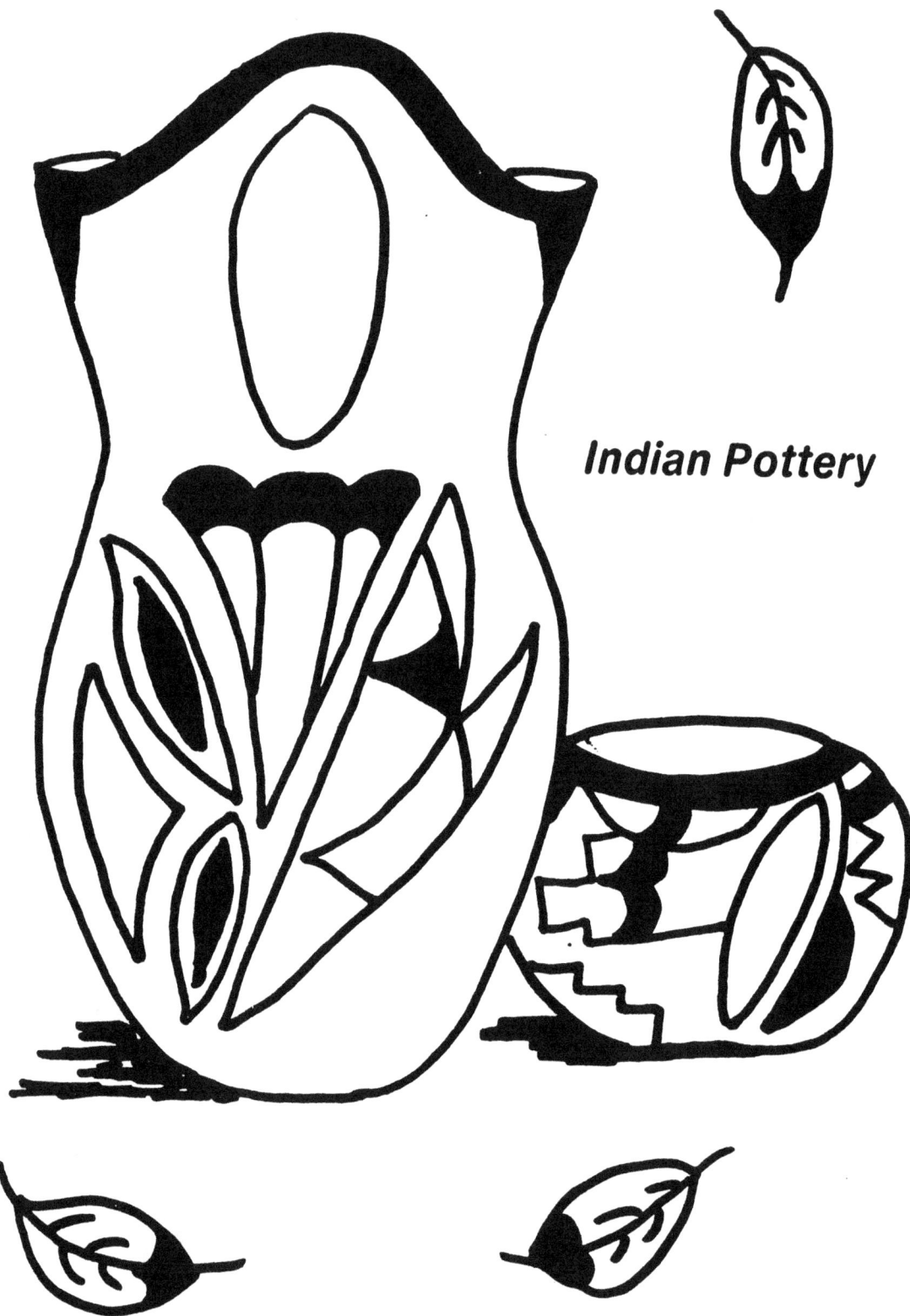

Indian Pottery

Mexican Pottery

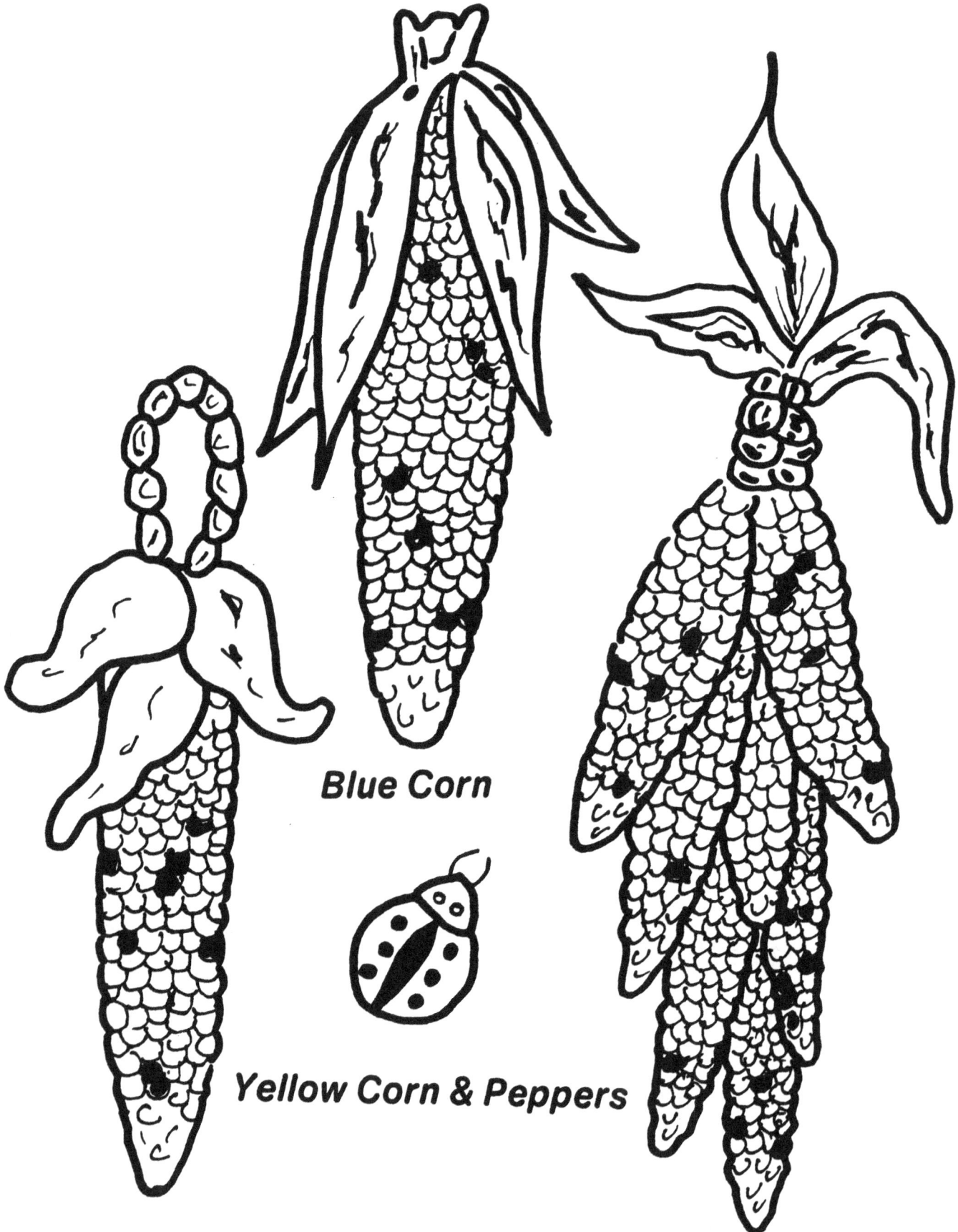

Blue Corn

Yellow Corn & Peppers

Christmas Ristra

Tree of Life - Mexico

Christmas Tree
- Mexico

Mexico

Ojos

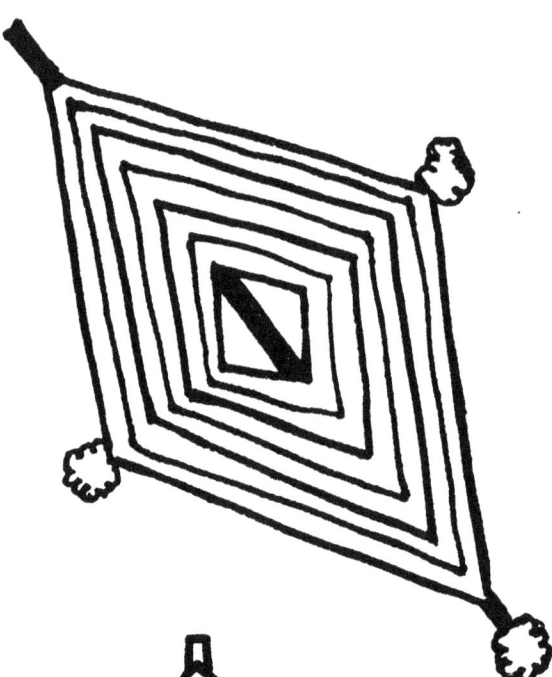

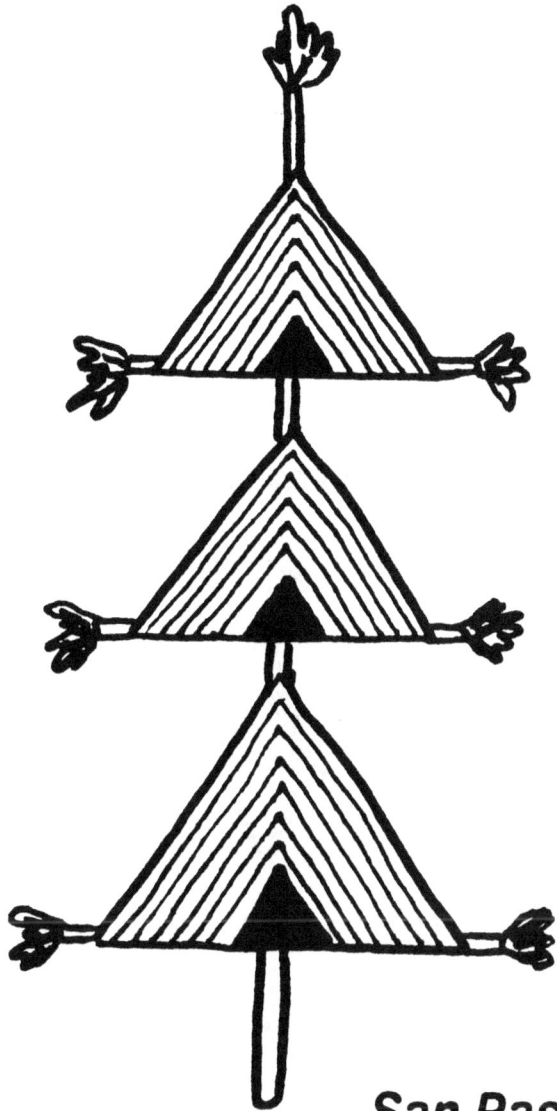

San Pasqual

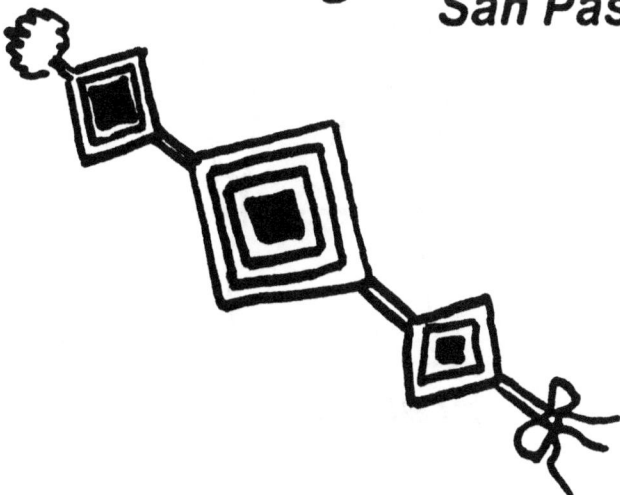

Some basic stitches you can use for the designs in this book.

Running Stitch

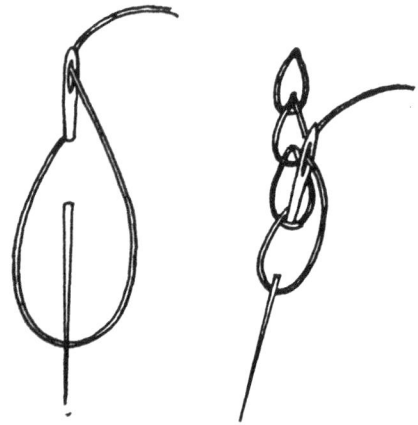

Chain Stitch

Stem Stitch

Slanted Satin Stitch

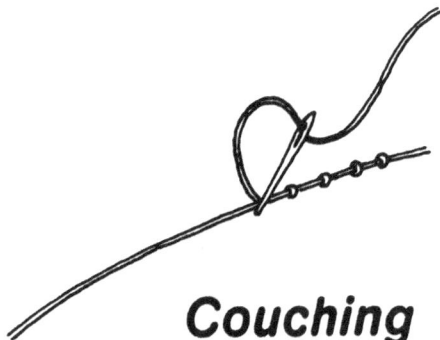

Couching

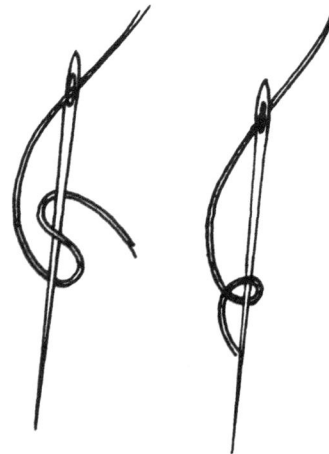

French Knot

BIBLIOGRAPHY

Allan, Richard. *Needlepoint Design Workbook.* New York: Service Communications, 1972

Appleton, LeRoy H. *American Indian Design and Decoration.* New York: Dover, 1971

Beagle, Peter. *American Denim: A New Folk Art.* New York: Abrams, 1975

Bowers, R.S. *Drawing and Design for Craftsmen.* Philadelphia: McKay (no date).

Cammann, Nora. *Needlepoint Designs from American Indian Art.* New York:
    Scribner, 1973

Chapman, Suzanne E. *Early American Design Motifs,* 2nd ed., rev. & enl.
    New York: Dover, 1974.

Christie, Archibald H. *Pattern Design: An Introduction to the Study of Formal Ornament.*
    New York: Dover, 1969

D'Amato, Janet, and D'Amato, Alex. *American Indian Craft Inspirations.*
    New York: Evans, 1972

Dorner, Gerd. *Folk Art of Mexico.* New York: Barnes, 1963.

Downer, Marion. *The Story of Design.* New York: Lothrop, Lee & Shepard, 1963.

Enciso, Jorge. *Design Motifs of Ancient Mexico.* New York: Dover, 1953.

Farleigh, John, *Design for Applied Decoration in the Crafts.* London: Bell, 1959.

Fewkes, Jesse Walter. *"Designs on prehistoric Hopi Pottery,"* pp. 207-284 in
    U.S. Bureau of American Ethnology, 33rd Annual Report. Washington: 1919.

Hallen, Julienne. *Folk Art Designs: American, Oriental, European.* New York:
    Homecrafts, 1949.

Hornung, Clarence Pearson. *Treasury of American Design; a pictorial survey of
    popular folk arts,* New York: Abrams, 1972.

Jessen, Ellen. *Ancient Peruvian Textile Design in Modern Stitchery.* New York:
    Van Nostrand Reinhold, 1972.

Lipman, Jean. *American folk Decoration.* New York: Dover, 1972.

Mera, Harry P. *Pueblo Indian Embroidery.* Santa Fe, New Mexico: Laboratory of
    Anthropology, 1943.

Miles, Walter. *Designs for Craftsmen: Textiles, Graphics, Ceramics, Wood, Glass, Metal,
Leather, and many other crafts.* Garden City, New York: Doubleday, 1962

Mirow, Gregory. *A Treasury of Design for Artists and Craftsmen.* New York: Dover, 1969.

Naylor, Maria. *Authentic Indian Designs: 2500 Illustrations from Reports of the Bureau
    of American Ethnology.* New York: Dover, 1975.

New Mexico Department of Vocational Education. *New Mexico Colonial Embroidery,* rev. ed. Santa Fe, New Mexico: 1943

Parker, Xenia Ley. *Designing for Crafts.* New York: Scribner, 1974.

Proctor, Richard M. *The Principles of Pattern for Craftsmen and Designers.* New York: Van Nostrand Reinhold, 1969.

Rogers, Gay Ann. *Tribal Designs for Needlepoint: 30 Original Designs Adapted from Eskimo, Polynesian and Indian Art.* Garden City, New York: Doubleday, 1977.

U.S. Works Progress Administration. *Federal Art Project, New Mexico. Portfolio of Spanish Colonial Design in New Mexico.* Santa Fe, New Mexico: 1937.

Wadsworth, Beula. *Design Motifs of the Pueblo Indians; with Applications in Modern Decorative Arts.* San Antonio: Naylor, 1957.

Wing, Frances S. *The Complete Book of Decoupage,* rev. ed. New York: Berkeley Pub., 1976.